Songs of t

To Rachel

with my very best wishes,

Andrew.

dp
THE DANEBURY PRESS

Songs of the Cross

Poems by Andrew Hawthorne

First published in 1995 by The Danebury Press
105B, Stour Road, Christchurch, Dorset BH23 1JN

ISBN 1 899665 00 5

Printed by Redwood Books Ltd., Trowbridge, Wiltshire

FOR CERI

if she wants it

Acknowledgements

Acknowledgements are due to the following: *English*, *Verse*, The Poetry Society, and The Oxford Union Society.

Thanks are also due to Peter Barry, C.H. Sisson, and R.S. Thomas, without whose kind encouragement these poems would not have been published.

Also to the Abbot and Monks of Elmore Abbey, Newbury, whose hospitality gave me opportunity to prepare the manuscript.

Preface

The crucifixion and the death of Christ were not just events which
happened to one man some 2000 years ago. They have universal
significance. Jesus, as God-become-man, suffered in his humanity the
lot of every man and woman. Each of us have Good Fridays of
anguish, whether they are physical, spiritual or emotional in origin.
And like Christ each of us will have to endure the Holy Saturday of
death.

The poems in this volume are an attempt to explore various facets
of crucifixion and death which are encountered in everyday life. They
are songs of suffering and lament, sung as it were to accompany the
experience of Christ's agony on that first Good Friday and Holy
Saturday.

At various points in the book Christ's song from the Cross or the
tomb appears, like the call of a fellow traveller across a mountain pass.
He is the traveller who has gone before us, who knows the landscape
of suffering and death but who has passed from its shadow into the
realm of new life. His final song, the anthem of Easter Day, finds
echoes in the second half of this collection and beckons us out of the
kingdom of death to share in his risen life.

About the Author

Andrew Hawthorne was born in 1968 in Andover, Hampshire, and
was educated locally there and at Jesus College, Oxford, where he
read modern history. He trained for the Anglican priesthood in
Chichester, at the same time as reading for a theology degree at
Southampton University. He is currently assistant curate at
Christchurch Priory, in Dorset.

He started writing poetry in 1986 and three years later received
recognition from the poet C.H. Sisson at a Poetry Society competition
in Oxford. His first published piece appeared in *English* in 1991. This
is his first volume of poetry.

He is married to Ceri, a teacher, and has a dog called Meg.

Contents

SATURDAY

THE THREE CHRISTCHURCH POEMS

Songs of the Cross

FRIDAY AFTERNOON

LAST LINES

You read in the paper of a dear friend's death.
Four lines to cradle and close his life.
What can be said? What can ever be said?
Begotten, beloved, to be buried.

THAW

Autumn's thaw, and in the stagnant water
The drowned leaf yields its bones
And pours the brown river of itself
Weeping into the mud.

THE APPLE TREE

The wheeze and crackle in the heat.
The summer is smoke now.
The embers glow in the moonlight.

HENGISTBURY HEAD

Your crumbling sides
Like a diary indifferently flicked through,
Diminished by revelation.

Ancient driftwood
A Saxon's careless spear
A horde of shells

Forgotten. At the tide's reach
Yesterday's secrets
For the casual eye
Written in the sand.

PIANO

You're a room with a locked piano
On a summer's evening. Forebidden melody

On the musty air: I pause
But with the echoes of my footsteps gone
Your music disappears behind the door.

THE TROUT

Quick shadow and a finger of water
Slips to the mayfly's wing. Second's turn
And you miss the beckoning but see
Its ripple of disappearance float downstream.

For E and A: A Sequence

I

SUMMER'S AFTERNOON

He loves me, he loves me not.
An hour spent counting petals
On a pleasant summer afternoon.
Fingers stained and a lapful
Of dead flowers.

II

PARTING KISS

It's midnight
And the violent storm of stars
Eternally cyclonic
Breaks over us,
Leaving our shadow awkward on the pavement.

III

LITANY

Our voices in the corn
Like a litany of perpetual vows.
You ask for a poem.
I am writing our epitaph.

IV

MEMORY

In each other's eyes
Twin rivers dreaming our neglected realities
In a gush of broken images. Too late:
An underused navigation.

Hands entwined, fingers inarticulate, our once discrete
And only conversation. Congress of desiccated bone
In an old vault. Splintered and brilliantly cold.

V

AFTERNOON

A sentimental, rainy afternoon
Against the window. A gentle wind
Gathering dead leaves,
Shadows crumbling over the glass.
We wait until the twilight fades
And our reflected eyes stare back
At our empty room.

VI

ACROSS THE WATER

Together we skim stones across the water.
We watch until their lines of ripples disappear.

They lie there
Safe, half immersed in mud.

VII

THE GARDEN

The darkness multiplies
The ghosts around your every breath,
So smooth.

Each rib, each curve,
Each somnambulistic move you make
To mark my gentle finger touch

Explodes a memory. Past loves,
Past nights,
Our past lives.

VIII

A Private Autumn

Blind, your sleeping hand finds mine.
A gentle squeeze
Like two leaves touching in the sun.

Tomorrow you won't remember this
And I won't tell you.
It's my little secret dream
In the palm of my hand,
Just between the two of us.

IX

THE WINDOW

The trains pass through the night.
The window rattles at their passing.

Sometimes you wake
And count the minutes between them.

X

THE BURDEN

Laughter as the burden grew. A full creel
At the first haul. Sunlight on the ocean bed.

Burst of water at the rope's end.
Seaweed and sand and an old bone.

XI

SHADOW

Your shadow lingers on the carpet,
Strays, reaches after mine.

And in the silence I catch
An echo of your passing voice
I love you, I love you.

XII

PHOTOGRAPH

The dust gathers on our photograph.
My fingers, too frail now,
Will not remove it.
Our eyes can't meet the way they used to.
Hand in hand we await the final blindness.

XIII

ANNIVERSARY

Your name is smooth
Beneath my fingertips.
I sit and lean against your headstone
And wonder who will come next year.

HOLOCAUST

Bosnia disintegrates in a corner
Of our living room. Smoke
And blood and bone nightly poured
In sacrifice: we number
The unintelligible dead. Then
The weather then
The welcome bed.

EYE

Dying, you were glad of an hour's peace,
The eye of your particular storm. Tempestuous

Time, rising to a fullness, flooding
Your mind
With a wash of frantic memories struggling,
Confused, like a netfull of landed fish, back
To the deep.

Too Late

Crab like, arthritic hands
Which seem to remember a rosary
Or a lover's face. In her burning head

A confession or that last
Moonlit assignation. Your eyes won't tell
What kind of love
Moves your lips to anxious pleas
Or your fingers to cling to your beloved,
Far too late.

WINTER DIG

Frostpick on bone: needles of ice
Piercing the marrow pores

And the frozen cry
As the frozen finger curls around its trowel
To disinherit and revive the clay;
Centuries of root twine and husk hermetic
In an intimate cell
Aired by a single slice: the second death.

WILL

Your anxious clawing hand
Strives to finish on paper

What you always considered left undone.
The final, emphatic scrawls like
Some erratic composer trying to tie
Those last elusive notes to the staveline.

Suddenly you're seized
By an unexpected attack:
Fingers clenched to a fist,
The pen dropped, that slowly
Ebbing ink.

RETURN

I shall return
To your faded wartime memories.
An empty ration book. Your photographs
Which smudge at the touch.
My inheritance

I am free now to forget.

LAMPLIGHT

Those hands you clasped so tight together
On that first embarrassed photograph,

Cool and gnarled in mine. As though
The sepia tint which blurred your early smile
Darkens in the dust and rubbings of the years,
Hides the shine, you say. You make me promise

To leave it hanging in your room,
Beneath the lamp which lights it so awkwardly.

Sepia Photograph

That sepia photograph so old
Your fingers browned to its touch. Her

Brittle, death bed smile forced
Like a spark from an anvil.

Memories blown like autumn leaves
Into a handful of dust.

THE DEAD LINE

At the sea's dead line
We erase with careful steps
Yesterday's writing on the sand,
Old worn epigrams in shells.

Hidden Talents

In your measured voice
Glint of deliberate iron:
Encrusted plough shard
Bleeding its rust into my palm,
The field's elusive dowry

And the tongue of generations
Lost in the soil. You worked
The furrow true and in the endless
Toil prospected for what your fathers
Never gave -

I wait. Dust settles. The shout
To the team that calls
To the homeward lane.
I hear the iron's thud
As it drops back to the earth.

OLD MILL

This almost indecipherable white-lettered facade:
Faint echoes from our great-grandfather's time

Impenetrable as turfed bone under
A Wiltshire longbarrow. We're no closer now
We've come to see these crumbling bricks

Than when we found
That old photo of his carting gang:
Blurred, surprised workmen
White with the spill of the flour

By which they plotted their way along
These awkward winding lanes.

AT A BURIAL

At the tomb's opening
The litany like the susurration of dead leaves.
Ponder the forgotten horde

Bone-creep and dust. And when you touched
(by God!) it was if they had never left you
But lingered on in their own mortality,
Overfilling the grave.

A SONG FOR THE MASTER

In his open palm
A fistful of iron
Dreaming in its rust
A premonition of the primal curse

The knifeblade and the coin.

This pleases me. To be the Father
Of several familiar generations, to see
The hands that scratched
From the stained chalk
My elusive but unforgiving gift:
I see the story repeated before it was begun.
Sing it again.

DANEBURY

Here beneath the gathering sky I find
The whispers of the ancient dead playing in my mind
Sifting through the rubble of countless seasons to uncover
A fragment of their bold bequest.

The wind seeps unsteadily over the downs
Sweeps the patient leaf hyperbolically
To a secret destination. Grasses,
Anonymous in multitudes, scythe the air
In gentle rhythms, roots seeking the grave.

Two Poems on the body of an Ice Age Man

I

Curse of this ice: my immaculate preservation.
To thaw is to pry: my last meal,
Colour of eyes, a unique finger print
The cut of my axe: the Ice Age personality.

How I yearn for the earth, its
Anonymity, disappearance of flesh
Stain of bone in the soil's palm
Or a grubby flint shard overlooked at their raking,
Sift of root crawl and worm, a proper death.

II

Parcelled between nations my flesh
Like wind-blown seed germinates
Beneath their carbon dating eyes.

My blind progeny. To seek only age
And diet: an irrelevant harvest.

Dig of scalpel's cold steel.
In their sterile fingers
The yield of my crop
(the warmth of kinship in the bone's cup,
premonition of their own humanity)
Prised like tares from a field of corn.
A second death.

WINCHESTER

These gothic dead. Our obeisance
At their chantry tombs: a fine, elusive monument.
Airy stone and a slim shaft of sunlight
Muted through the glass. Their features

Obliterated with furious care, cosmetics
Of indiscrete history, an ambiguous epitaph.
We smooth our palms over their evasive faces
And claim the dust within the stone.

ROMSEY ABBEY

"When opened, her tomb not only contained human
remains, but also the traces of a flower."

Our kinship of bone knob and flower:
A faded rose,
Dust in the prying palm. The
Inconsistent dead

In muted resurrection. Echoes
Of old Latin on the choirboy's tongue,
An elusive etymology. Sharp cut lines
On the hatchment plate.

QUERN

The growl of the angry quern
Floods my mind:

I hear your tumbled comments
On the harvest,
How the August fire ripened it
Until it cried to be gathered;

How the ox and the barn and your hands
Nearly broke with it
And the lanes gilded with the spill;

And how you buried a little urn of it
Secretly one smokefall for the blessings
Of your father and mother from the field,
Then offered thanks at the ooze of the flour
Over the mill floor.

And now the barley comes quick from your own grave.

GLENCOE

Echoes of ancient war. Clash of shattered steel
And the tincture of blood on stone and heather.
The screech

Of the lonely rook and the babble of the stream
Where the swords were washed after the slaughter
Mingle with the cry of your plaintive bones
Long scattered in the soil.

MARKINGS

I heard your whispers count
The undoing days around the roots
of bowing grasses

You had often walked this way, to carry
Your pail of frozen water home
To melt the work's grime

Earth and root slime and the dust
Of old bones compounded anonymously
And swept with the strife of the plough
Over huge distances

Only the tramp of a dozen generations
Kept it clear; and when the pail spilt
It revealed brown mirrors in the stones
And was quick to seep through.

MY DOG MEG

With her almost human eyes
My cunning dog lies
Inviting atavistic vowels.
In exchange
She'll flick her ancient tail
And shake a tired paw

And remember you.

ANNUNCIATION

Your old fanciful annunciation comes back to us
Like a nodule of old bone found on the grazing.
Sun bleached, plough chipped
Promising to prophesy our deprivation, water
And blood to their old home. See how it warms
As we turn it in the light.

The Wind in the Trees

We dream an ocean in the trees.
We walk beneath,
Two shipwrecked dead,
Wondering if this is all we will bequeath.

KISSING BONES

I raise you to my lips
For the first time.

The slow fleshing of the years,
A smooth yet insubstantial alibi.

Often in my dream we would lie here.
The moss has grown in the meantime
And the words become indecipherable.

We withdraw. We never knew.
We danced to a tune
That was the echo of a lost sound.

CHOICES

It will come sure enough.
In an eloquent swirl of dust
Or a ripple from a drowning stone.

And if you catch it right
You will perpetuate the choice
And leave the answer for another man.

In a Monastery Garden

Even the bloom of the vespers echo in the nave
Cannot summon such imagery
Nor the turn of the illuminated page

Or the hush before benediction.
In the dusk
The failing sun-play, faint on root and stone

The gold leaf-fall, immense
Swirling a host of memories to the earth.

O God, what am I
That I should be mirrored in the infolded death
Of a late November afternoon?

Songs of the Cross

SATURDAY

The Three Christchurch Poems

I

DAWN: THE FIRST HOUR

Pig's blood and gold:
Common elements of prayer.

A solemn, myopic invocation
At the first stroke; muttered curse
And contrition. A new devotion
At your fingertips.

Between the beech wood and paint
Salvation and pain seared, martyrs'
Vocation at the workbench
In a shaft of sunlight.

Then varnish and blessing.
A dream of saints
In glorious apotheosis.

II

SCRIPTORIUM

The grind of the bone and the black pig's blood
Mixed with the sulphuric curses of a dozen previous attempts

Ooze over the bleached vellum. Word
After precise liturgical word
Filling the page like the precentor's voice
Overfilling the quire.

Soon the moment for the lead guidelines to be eased away
And the delicate application of the beaten gold
To be followed by a wash of lapis lazuli
And emerald: the all-important initial letter
The carcass of the text

Complete. Then the drying, the cut of the straight edge
The prayer of dedication at the altar,
The murmur of thanksgiving at the turn of the page.

III

THE URGENT CONTRACT

Brothers on the scaffold,
Mason and glazier, tracery
And glass, finger and file
Weaving an intimate tapestry.

Dawn to dawn, catching each mood
Of the sun or the moon in rising glass
Panel by panel translating light to liturgy.

Bloodshot eyes, monosyllables
Echoing into the vaulting
Moonshadow at play on the pillars

Ease of the last lead
Jointing glass to stone, two
Quick prayers of dedication,
Feel the flood of the nave at first light.

SIMON

A mocking silence, and your prayers
Cupped into splintered hands fail
Even to form an echo in your palm.

By the faded images of that old predictable story
He recasts the broken parable in new words
Breathed into the scorching sun.

Hollow prayers. Those splinters bite
As flesh stains iron, clenched fists
To clasp and crush his agony. Small extinguished
Chance. See the blood streak across the dust.

ORGAN PRACTICE

for M.S.

I sit beneath the choirscreen
And let your tide of music lap over me.
It's pleasant
Counting notes in perfect anonymity
Into an ocean of prayer.

PRAYER

The old palmfuls of air
Squeezed into familiar meaning
Come back to us, waiting
For resuscitation. Clusters
Of April leaves, fragments drawn
From recurrent memories of death.
See how each unfurls
In the morning sun.

Obituary

Scratching in the sand
Your own obituary. Read
What you will.

A woman forgiven.
A half obliterated message
Under the accusers' feet.